A FRIEND IN THE LIBRARY

HOME-LIFE

BY

EVA MARCH TAPPAN

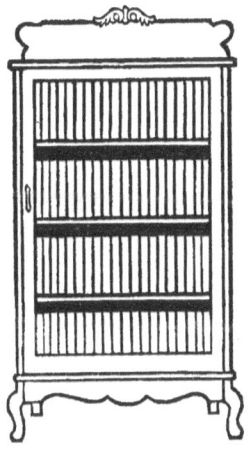

British Library Cataloguing-in-Publication Data
A catalogue record for this book is available from the
British Library

HOME-LIFE

A FRIEND IN THE LIBRARY

A Practical Guide to the Writings of

RALPH WALDO EMERSON

NATHANIEL HAWTHORNE

HENRY WADSWORTH LONGFELLOW

JAMES RUSSELL LOWELL

JOHN GREENLEAF WHITTIER

OLIVER WENDELL HOLMES

IN TWELVE VOLUMES

VOLUME III

Eva March Tappan

Eva March Tappan was born on 26th December 1854 in Blackstone, Massachusetts, America. She is well known as a factual as well as fictional writer, but spent her early career as a teacher. Tappan was the only child of Reverend Edmund March Tappan and Lucretia Logée, and received her education at the esteemed Vassar College. This was a private coeducational liberal arts college, in the town of Poughkeepsie, New York, from which she graduated in 1875. Here, Tappan was a member of Phi Beta Kappa, the oldest honour society for the liberal arts and sciences, widely considered as the nations most prestigious society. She also edited the *Vassar Miscellany,* a college publication.

After leaving her early education, Tappan began teaching at Wheaton College, one of the oldest institutions of higher education for women in the United States, founded in 1834 and based in Norton, Massachusetts. She taught Latin and German here, from 1875 until 1880, before moving on to the Raymond Academy in Camden, New Jersey where she was associate Principal until 1894. Tappan also received a graduate degree in English Literature from the University of Pennsylvania. This allowed her to pursue her first love, that of reading and writing, and she taught as head of the English department at the English High School at Worcester, Massachusetts.

It was only after this date that Tappan began her literary career, writing about famous characters in history, often aimed at educating children in important historical themes and epochs. Some of her better known works include, *In the Days of William the Conqueror* (1901) and *In the Days of Queen Elizabeth* (1902), *The Out-of-Door Book* (1907), *When Knights Were Bold* (1911) and *The Little Book of the Flag* (1917). Tappan never married, being a happy singleton, and died on 29th January 1930, aged seventy-five.

HOME-LIFE

IT sounds exceedingly broad-minded and liberal and independent to hear any one say, "I am a citizen of the world"; but most people have all they can do to be good citizens of even one small town, and I am not sure but it is better to be a good citizen of a home than of a town. Those intrepid old Jesuit missionaries who braved the horrors of captivity and torture that they might preach the Word to the savages of the New World, had for their motto "Ubique," — *wheresoever;* but with all their earnest faith and their joy in the work that they were doing, they must have longed sometimes for the homes of their boyhood on earth as well as for those that they hoped to find in the life to come. Maybe the thought of heaven owes more of its attractiveness than one always realizes to that one phrase, "many mansions." Supposing it had read "many boarding-houses," or tenements, or apartments! We could get on very well without golden streets and pearly gates, but what would make up for the loss of the "many mansions," — many homes? Bayard Taylor roamed the world over, but with the longing for a home ever in his heart. Clearer to Scott than any scene in his romances was the vision of the home for which he was working. "The love of home is interwoven with all that is pure and deep and lasting in earthly affection," says Longfellow ("Outre-Mer," 324).

Home is a refuge, a fourth dimension of space into which one may vanish at will, and in it find comfort and joy, whether the world outside goes right or wrong. And after one has closed the door of home behind him and wandered out into the world, what a joy and what a safeguard it is to be able to look back to a home of happiness and beauty! The remembrance of it is a touchstone of pleasures. The light from its windows, shining upon unworthy amusements and aims, cannot fail to reveal their true character in all its cheapness and tawdriness.

No home is too small or too poor for peace and beauty. A veil of morning glories shading the glaring windows is better than lace curtains. A flash of nasturtiums on the stone wall is finer than any painted canvas. A rose or a honeysuckle running over the doorway gives a more cordial welcome than a silver salver.

A FRIEND IN THE LIBRARY

As Whittier says ("Among the Hills," i. 260), —

> How rich
> And restful even poverty and toil
> Become when beauty, harmony, and love
> Sit at their humble hearth as angels sat
> At evening in the patriarch's tent, when man
> Makes labor noble.

A little farther on in the same poem is a picture of the home that is not a home: —

> I look
> Across the lapse of half a century,
> And call to mind old homesteads, where no flower
> Told that the spring had come, but evil weeds,
> Nightshade and rough-leaved burdock, in the place
> Of the sweet doorway greeting of the rose
> And honeysuckle, where the house-walls seemed
> Blistering in the sun, without a tree or vine
> To cast the tremulous shadow of its leaves
> Across the curtainless windows.

4

The people who lived in such forlorn home-lessness might be

Rich in broad woodlands and in half-tilled fields,
And yet so pinched and bare and comfortless,
The veriest straggler, limping on his rounds,
The sun and air his sole inheritance,
Laughed at a poverty that paid its taxes,
And hugged his rags in self-complacency!

Whittier gives a contrasting picture and tells the story — a true one — of the coming of a city maiden to the country of the Bear-camp: —

From school and ball and rout she came,
  The city's fair, pale daughter,
To drink the wine of mountain air
  Beside the Bearcamp Water.

The hero of the story is the manly young farmer who woos and wins her.

And so the farmer found a wife,
His mother found a daughter:
There looks no happier home than hers
On pleasant Bearcamp Water.

Flowers spring to blossom where she walks
The careful ways of duty;
Our hard, still lines of life with her
Are flowing curves of beauty.

And as for the farmer, —

How dwarfed against his manliness
She sees the poor pretension,
The wants, the aims, the follies, born
Of fashion and convention!

A young man who has grown up in such a home goes out into the world shielded from many of its troubles, armed to meet many of its battles. In homes like these lies the strength of our country; here is the foundation of patriotism. The early Romans never thought of being paid for defending their country; they drove away invaders from the land as they would have driven away robbers from their dwellings.

Love of fatherland is only love of home grown deeper and broader. Lowell says (xv. 100), "There is something magnificent in having a country to love." When he was in England, Leslie Stephens insisted (xvi. 332) that "one main charm of the Land's End to him was that nothing intervened between it and Massachusetts."

I wonder if every one realizes how beautifully Longfellow's "Building of the Ship" (i. 277) brings out the thought that love of country follows naturally upon love of home. In the poem, a merchant bids the Master build him

        A goodly vessel,
That shall laugh at all disaster,
  And with wave and whirlwind wrestle!

The merchant's word
Delighted the Master heard;
For his heart was in his work, and the heart
Giveth grace unto every Art.

Beside the Master stood

The fiery youth, who was to be
The heir of his dexterity,
The heir of his house, and his daughter's hand,
When he had built and launched from land
What the elder head had planned.

The day of the launching of the ship Union is to be also the wedding day; and when it has come, —

The prayer is said,
The service read,
The joyous bridegroom bows his head.

The illustration, the simile, the picture, is the building and launching of a "goodly vessel"; but the deeper significance of the poem is the making of a home. Longfellow says elsewhere ("The Hanging of the Crane," iii. 193):—

> O fortunate, O happy day,
> When a new household finds its place
> Among the myriad homes of earth,
> Like a new star just sprung to birth.

But the meaning is twofold. Longfellow thinks not only of the one home, but of the many that make up our country, and he closes with his magnificent apostrophe beginning, —

> Thou, too, sail on, O Ship of State!
> Sail on, O Union, strong and great!

A FRIEND IN THE LIBRARY

Humanity with all its fears,
With all the hopes of future years,
Is hanging breathless on thy fate!

Whittier's "Snow-Bound" (ii. 134) is the most perfect picture that we have of country life in the early part of the nineteenth century. Here Whittier was at his best, for he was writing of the life of his childhood, of the home and friends that he loved. This is his picture of the fireplace of the olden time: —

Shut in from all the world without,
We sat the clean-winged hearth about,
Content to let the north-wind roar
In baffled rage at pane and door,
While the red logs before us beat
The frost-line back with tropic heat;
And ever, when a louder blast
Shook beam and rafter as it passed,

The merrier up its roaring draught
The great throat of the chimney laughed;
The house-dog on his paws outspread
Laid to the fire his drowsy head,
The cat's dark silhouette on the wall
A couchant tiger's seemed to fall;
And, for the winter fireside meet,
Between the andirons' straddling feet,
The mug of cider simmered slow,
The apples sputtered in a row,
And, close at hand, the basket stood
With nuts from brown October's wood.

About the fireplace, while the wind roars and the snow piles up in huge drifts, the snow-bound family sit and tell tales of shipwrecks, of Indian raids, — for the days of Indian warfare were not far distant, — of the struggles of the early Quakers, of the huskings and the apple-bees and the sleigh-rides of long ago. The college boy —

Brisk wielder of the birch and rule,
The master of the district school —

teases the cat, sings college songs, and tells stories of life in Dartmouth's classic halls. Some one has said that the chief value of an act lies in its being pleasant to remember; and certainly a family that has sat together about a fireplace has stored away one of the best and dearest of memories.

Lowell declares ("Pope," ii. 461) that "if God made poets for anything, it was to keep alive the traditions of the pure, the holy, and the beautiful"; and certainly Lowell magnifies his office, for no one keeps alive the traditions of love of home more tenderly than he. When he was a junior at Harvard, he wrote to a friend (xiv. 19), "As I run about over the same familiar spots which I trod in joyous, careless infancy, my heart leaps again, and the innocent days of my childhood come over me like a dream." This was good honest feeling, but little more than eight years had passed since this world-weary young collegian was rejoicing because his mother had promised him "any sort of buttons" he might choose for his "new suit of blue broadcloth clothes to wear every day and to play in"; and it *is* funny to find him writing of his early innocence when probably the worst sin of his mature youth was his making rhymes when his father wished him to be studying his lessons. In the Introduction to the "Biglow Papers" (x. 31), he gives a rhymed account of his early school-days. He says:—

Ah, dear old times! there once it was my hap,
Perched on a stool, to wear the long-eared cap;

From books degraded, there I sat at ease,
A drone, the envy of compulsory bees.

If he wore the dunce-cap only once, he must have been a pretty good child. He was not at all like a certain small boy of to-day who would not refrain from asking "the next fellow" for a knife for the sake of wearing home "a cent on a string," as he scornfully proclaimed; for this little scholar of three-quarters of a century ago was glad of even medals.

Rewards of merit, too, full many a time,
Each with its woodcut and its moral rhyme,
And pierced half-dollars hung on ribbons gay
About my neck (to be returned next day),
I carried home, rewards as shining then
As those that deck the lifelong pains of men,
More solid than the redemanded praise
With which the world beribbons later days.

There is a special fascination about looking

back to the childhood of famous people; for we are not reconciled to the thought of their having been ordinary children. We expect to find at least a remarkable poem or two among their childish scribblings, or in their letters some phrase that suggests a walking in ways that are not those of ordinary mortals. How fortunate it is that so little is known of Shakespeare's childhood! Otherwise, fond mammas and devoted child-students would be more painfully on the alert than ever for the traits that indicate genius. Whittier has left us a picture of himself in his "Barefoot Boy" (ii. 126), and we can imagine the serious-faced, dark-eyed little Quaker sitting with his

Bowl of milk and bread;
Pewter spoon and bowl of wood,
On the door-stone, gray and rude.

The old customs were dear to the Quaker poet. His "Telling the Bees" (i. 186) is founded upon one of them, the superstition that if a death has taken place in the house and the bees are not informed and their hives draped with black, they will fly away in search of a new home. In Whittier's poem, —

> Before them [the hives], under the garden wall,
>   Forward and back,
> Went drearily singing the chore-girl small.

The song that she sang was, —

> Stay at home, pretty bees, fly not hence!
> Mistress Mary is dead and gone!

Longfellow has sometimes been called "the least national" of our poets; but the man who could write "The Building of the Ship" had surely no lack of patriotism. He loved the richness of culture of the lands across the seas; but he never failed to feel ("In Memoriam," Emerson, ix. 261)

> The loyal tie
> Which holds to home 'neath every sky.

From Longfellow, too, comes one of the tenderest of our home songs ("Song," iii. 125): —

> Stay, stay at home, my heart, and rest;
> Home-keeping hearts are happiest,
> For those that wander they know not where
> Are full of trouble and full of care;
> To stay at home is best.

Longfellow's home was the fine old Tory mansion in which he boarded during the days of his early professorship at Harvard. Some of the poems that he wrote about his home-life have become such favorites that thousands who have never entered the house feel as if it were an old friend. Best known of them all is

"The Children's Hour" (iii. 63), that twilight "pause in the day's occupations" when the little folk might invade at their will even the study of their poet father.

Long before this poem was written, sorrow had made its way into the happy home; one little daughter had gone from him. In his diary Longfellow wrote, "An inappeasable longing to see her comes over me at times, which I can hardly control." To the poet, however, had been given not only the trustfulness that brings comfort, but also the talent to interpret the comfort that he had found so that it might bring help to others. His " Resignation" (i. 303), which he wrote about the death of his own child, has consoled thousands who sorrowed. The grief of many an aching heart has been softened by his —

She is not dead, — the child of our affection, —
    But gone unto that school
Where she no longer needs our poor protection,
    And Christ himself doth rule.

Several years earlier he had written "The Reaper and the Flowers" (i. 20), another poem of comforting. Longfellow's belief in a future life was marked by a quiet certainty which soothes and helps in a time of sorrow. He did not reason about the "recognition of friends in heaven," but said of the bereaved mother, —

    She knew she should find them all again
      In the fields of light above.

One of the most touching of Longfellow's poems of sympathy is "The Two Angels" (iii. 28). One of the poet's daughters was born at the time of the death of Lowell's wife, and Longfellow writes of the two angels, one of Life and one of Death, who passed over the village. At his door the angel of Life entered "with a smile, that filled the house with light"; but

'T was at thy door, O friend! and not at mine,
   The angel with the amaranthine wreath,
Pausing, descended, and with voice divine
   Whispered a word that had a sound like Death.

Some years after this, the same sorrow came to Longfellow in the loss of his beloved wife. It was of this that he wrote "The Cross of Snow" (iii. 242), which was found in his portfolio after his own death.

Holmes says, "A poet wants a home. He can dispense with an apple-parer and a reaping machine." In Holmes's "Our Hundred Days in Europe" (x. 116), he declares that in America we have no real homes, we "only encamp," and our houses are soon torn down or altered beyond recognition. Nevertheless, the jocund young traveler of seventy-seven summers had an honest affection for the home of his youth, if it was a mere encampment. He tells us ("The Poet at the Breakfast-Table," ii. 247) of the Star-of-Bethlehem that used to grow in the southwest corner of the front yard, and how, after much wandering in foreign lands and learning "to think in the words of strange people," he went back to that front yard and searched through the tall grass to find the slender leaves of the little plant.

Much like Holmes's pleasure in discovering the Star-of-Bethlehem of his early memories was Lowell's delight when, after becoming famous on both sides of the ocean and being minister at the Court of St. James, he returned to Cambridge and his dearly beloved Elmwood. He forbids (xvi. *passim*) the fallen leaves to be raked away, for their rustling brings early memories to mind; he studies the elms in front of the house and notes that they are "a trifle thicker in the waist, perhaps, as is the wont of prosperous elders," and says that they are a balm to his eyes. He declares that the trees all know him and will take heart again now that he has returned. In another place (xv. 363), he writes, "A horse-chestnut, of which I planted the seed more than fifty years ago, lifts its huge stack of shade before me and loves me with all its leaves." He sends letters back to Europe about his dogs lying before the fire, and "looking round at me from time to time," he says, "lest I should forget they love me." He writes of even the mice in the walls, and tells his friend that he assists at their little tragedies and comedies behind the wainscot in the night hours and builds up plots in his fancy. "'T is a French company," he states learnedly, "for I hear them distinctly say *wee, wee* sometimes. . . . I overheard an elopement the other night behind the wainscot, and the solicitors talking with the desolated husband afterwards. It was very exciting. Ten thousand grains of corn damages." Anything that was alive, whether plant or animal, appealed to Lowell. His observations of the birds are most sympathetic and also most accurate, and he was "next friend" to all those that built in his Elmwood trees. At times it was somewhat of a question whether he or they were owner of the place. He says ("My Garden Acquaintance," i. 257) : —

All my birds look upon me as if I were a mere tenant at will, and they were landlords. With shame I confess it, I have been bullied even by a humming-bird. This spring, as I was cleansing a pear-tree of its lichens, one of those little zigzag-ging blurs came purring toward me, couching his long bill like a lance, his throat sparkling with angry fire, to warn me off from a Missouri currant whose honey he was sipping.

Hawthorne was radiantly happy in his home, so happy that he was almost afraid, "for there is something more awful in happi-ness than in sorrow," he says (xviii. 450), "the latter being earthly and finite, the former composed of the substance and texture of eternity, so that spirits still embodied may well tremble at it." Even the most matter-of-fact pages of his journal ("American Note-Books," xviii) are overflowing with his joy. "How sweet it was to draw near my own home," he writes (xviii. 368), "after having lived homeless in the world so long!" And then he gives a minute account of the "Old Manse" as it was at first, "with its gable and crossbeams, its high-backed, short-legged, rheumatic chairs, small, old tables, bedsteads with lofty posts, stately chests of drawers, looking-glasses in antique black frames." Following this is the cheerier picture of the home as Hawthorne had made it, with his "gladsome carpet" and "cheerful paint," new furniture, pictures, and flowers. He declares himself convinced that the spirit of its

former owner will never haunt it, so changed
has it become. "Probably the ghost gave
one peep into it, uttered a groan, and van-
ished forever," he decides comfortably; but
he was not fully convinced, for he fancied he
had heard "a sound as of some person crum-
pling paper in his hand," and this must have
been the former ministerial occupant with one
of his sermons! But if there are no real ghosts
about the Old Manse, there are at least
dreams and fancies without number. The
apple trees are "part of the family." "One
tree is harsh and crabbed, another mild; one
is churlish and illiberal, another exhausts
itself with its free-hearted bounties." The
pond-lilies in the river that flows at the end of
the orchard shrink away "with sweet prudish-
ness, beyond the grasp of mortal arm." He

went for a walk and met Emerson, who said,
"There were Muses in the woods to-day, and
whispers to be heard in the breezes." He
wonders whether it troubled Adam "to see his
fruits decaying on the ground, after he had
watched them through the sunny days of the
world's first summer." He wants a dog and a
kitten, and feels it his duty to support a pig,
even if he has "no design of feasting upon
him." By and by, the golden glamour around
even the commonest things suddenly vanishes,
for his wife has gone to pay a visit, and he is
left alone with the kitten, who came to him,
"talking with the greatest earnestness," and
a maid who slams doors like thunder-claps.
He goes rowing with Thoreau, he is "on the
point of choking with a huge German word,"
he gazes despairingly at "an immense joint

of roast veal," which the door-slamming maiden has placed before him in his loneliness. "These solitary meals are the dismalest part of my present experience," he moans. For two whole days he speaks not a word to any one. What a welcome Mrs. Hawthorne must have received when the visit came to an end! That page of the journal was sacred to her, and is not for us to read; but I fancy that Lowell has put into two lines what Hawthorne felt, what every one who has a happy home must know, however vaguely and indistinctly ("The Dead House," xii. 220): —

> To learn such a simple lesson,
> Need I go to Paris and Rome,
> *That the many make the household,*
> *But only one the home ?*

HOME-LIFE

ADDITIONAL

LOWELL

After the Burial, xii. 218.
Irene, ix. 10.
My Love, ix. 18.
The Changeling, ix. 251.

EMERSON

Domestic Life, vii. 103.

WHITTIER

The Homestead, i. 413.
My Playmate, i. 238.

LONGFELLOW

Haunted Houses, iii. 23.
To-morrow, iii. 146.
Evangeline, ii. 17.
Footsteps of Angels, i. 24.
To a Child, i. 230.
The Old Clock on the Stair, i. 256.
The Open Window, i. 309.
Twilight, i. 294.

QUESTIONS

1. Wherein lies the value of Whittier's "Among the Hills" (i. 265)?

   In its poetical beauty, its truth, and its picturing of a happy home in which husband and wife are the complement of each other.

2. What is the foundation of the strength of our country?

   Its homes.

3. What is the twofold significance of Longfellow's "The Building of the Ship" (i. 277)?

   The founding of a new household and the making of a country.

4. Where may the best picture of country life in the early part of the nineteenth century be found?

   In Whittier's "Snow-Bound" (ii. 134).

5. What does Lowell declare is the mission of the poet?

"To keep alive the traditions of the pure, the holy, and the beautiful."

6. Where does Lowell describe his early school-days?

In the Introduction to the "Biglow Papers" (ii).

7. Where may a picture of Whittier's boyhood be found?

In his "Barefoot Boy" (ii. 126).

8. Name one of the most tender of the songs of home.

Longfellow's "Stay, stay at home, my heart, and rest" (iii. 125).

9. Why do strangers feel so tender an interest in Longfellow's home?

Because of his "Children's Hour" (iii. 63), and other poems of his home-life.

10. Why are Longfellow's poems of sympathy so great a comfort to those in sorrow?

    Because he had the power to interpret for others the comfort that he himself had found.

11. What was the foundation of Longfellow's poem "The Two Angels" (iii. 8)?

    The fact that the birth of one of his daughters and the death of Lowell's wife occurred on the same day.

12. What is the special charm in Lowell's love of home?

    His frank childlikeness in writing of the smallest details.

13. Where was Hawthorne's first home after his marriage?

    At the "Old Manse" in Concord, Mass.

14. Where may the description of his life at the Old Manse be found?

HOME-LIFE

In the "American Note-Books" (xviii), and in the first chapter of his "Mosses from an Old Manse" (iv, v).

15. Where may extracts from Mrs. Hawthorne's letters about life in the Old Manse be found?

    In the Introductory Note to the "Mosses."

16. What famous lines from Lowell (xii. 220) express most perfectly the home spirit?

    "The many make the household,
    But only one the home."